The Lizard Thieves

Love Poems

Amy Beth Katz

Living Dreams Press

The Lizard Thieves © 2012 by Amy Beth Katz.
All rights reserved.

Living Dreams Press
1st Ed., First Printing, May 2012.

Cover design by Brad Katz and Amy Beth Katz.
Cover photograph by Michael Turco.

Library of Congress Cataloging-in Publication Data
Katz, Amy Beth, 1968-
  The Lizard Thieves: Love Poems. -- 1st ed.

Library of Congress Control Number: 2012908057
ISBN-13: 978-0615639918
ISBN-10: 0615639917

Printed in the United States of America.

Living Dreams Press
3890 Pueblo Ave C
Santa Barbara, CA 93110
www.livingdreamspress.com

"All, all is theft,
all is unceasing and rigorous competition in nature;
the desire to make off with the substance of others is the
foremost - the most legitimate - passion nature has bred into us
and, without doubt, the most agreeable one."

~ *Marquis de Sade*

To the hungry ones...

LE MENU

I. Forked-Tongue In Cheek

LE MENU

II. Eat Prey, Love

LE MENU

III. *The Violence of Feathers*

LE MENU

IV. Swallow Me, Holy

Part I. Forked Tongue In Cheek

A forked tongue is a <u>tongue</u> split into two distinct tines at the tip; this is a feature common to many species of <u>reptiles</u>. Reptiles <u>smell</u> using the tip of their tongue, and a forked tongue allows them to sense from which direction a smell is coming. Sensing from both sides of the head and following trails based on chemical cues is called <u>tropotaxis</u>.[1] It is unclear whether or not forked tongued reptiles can actually follow trails or if this is just a hypothesis.[2][3][4]

www.wikipedia.org

Aragorn: Are you frightened?
Frodo: Yes.
Aragorn: Not nearly frightened enough. I know what hunts you.

~ Lord of the Rings
`

Sonnet of Ribbits

They french with frog-like Ribbits, quivering
warriors croaking queer moans, him driving
hard her home on crimson wool ascribing
to amphibian games. She shivering against night's
forked tongue which flicks from shank to shin.
"Am I a popsicle gone freezer burned?"
She yearns to ask, but doesn't. Trust unearned
turns lust to pain. But happily, pain is warm. Wet
grass finds buttock strayed while shoulder blades
saw at gritty blanket dried-blood colored
under moon-shy sky and goose-flesh tryst. "Beds
are absurd. I've not slept in mine for days."

Toads and snakes shed skin by rubbing something hard;
she kisses him, liking his tree-bark beard.

O Anna O

O Anna O,
your crime was your clitoris.
Your illness the spontaneous combustion of lust
suffered in an era when Victoria
wore a thrown instead of a thong
and was locked in a fortress
of her own stays and bones
instead of her lingerie drawer
where young women in the free world
live now.

You tried to scream state secrets
in tongues forked with tines designed to steal
bites of ambrose off of Eros's plate.

In another age you might have been a sex goddess
Marilyn or Lady Ga Ga or a Pentecostal,
the Oracle of Delphi, a doll
of some distant ventriloquist in the clouds
or a poet laureate.
You didn't need electric shock therapy,
or to be immersed in ice, or tied down to a bed
(unless the straps were silk,

and the only thing oppressing you was a lover's
naked thrusts, as in the story of another O.)

All you needed was a translator with a cock
that crowed
and you found one
in the good doctor who brewed you
a warm cup of crazy.

You drank this diagnosis together
over High Tea
and poetry.

Later when his ears grew pointy
and his fox felt cured,
he battered his hysterical chicken in sanity,
so sane you were.

(Like a baptist minister
declares each man a sinner,
dunks him like a Lipton tea bag in hot water,
and he come out tasting saved.)

When you became pregnant
with his vocabulary and desire
he began to worry and questioned the paternity

of his fame.
He threw out the baby
but kept the bathwater.
He bottled and patented it, in his name
only
he dubbed you insane
which could only mean
you were.

But the healing potion retained your scent;
the world remembered that a rose by any other
name wouldn't smell as sweet,
so they remembered yours
even though it wasn't yours, was never yours
a pen-name tattooed on your fate
by another writer's hand
like a prisoner's number engraved in his flesh
by the executioners of a death camp.

Your associations grew
like history's tea roses
laced with rhinoceros thorns.
This is where the horned doctors dwelled
and still do, somewhere
between the prick and the blossom.

O Anna O,
when you flowered and they pricked
your fingers and inflations
to study the patterns of red
chrysanthemums,
did you enjoy bleeding for them?

You certainly did not wilt!

Did they need to pry
open your veins with a crow bar,
or did you caw for more
(like I do?)

Did you saunter around their offices
in your revealing freudian slip
and search lustful eyes in the looking glasses
to see if they had anything to reflect
when you suggested, dryly,
"Some vampires drink words"?

O Anna O,
he discovered talk therapy,
but you invented it
like God invented electricity.

In an early experiment, Ben Franklin
stuck a chicken on a spit and roasted it by churning
it over and over with electricity.

I think of you every time
insight strikes me like lightening
during a fifty minute hour
and the man behind the couch
takes credit cards.

I think of you every time
I raise my slashed wrist
to my analyst's lips,
and when I slip
my electric tongue
into his foxy
ear.

I think of you every time
I usurp a thrown
and wear a crown of thorns
in my wild
hair.

Arms For Sale

I went to see an Arms Dealer
because I needed a hug.
He tried to sell me a Kalashnikov
with a pair of bazookas;
I told him I wasn't into Russian lesbians.

The studly mannequin in the gun shop window
was dressed in leather and camo
possibly indicating a bondage fetish.

So I whispered in his sexy, latex ear,
"Free me from my freedom!
Independence is a capital quality
but far too taxing
and I'm saving up to buy love."

It's true,
I use to be strong.
But strength is a heavy burden --
It's weakened me.
Now, I'm meek like a mouse
who has tricked the trap
but is hunted
by the cheese.

"Relinquish me from liberty!
Your arms are worthy chains."

I turned to the arms dealer, and pleaded,

"Our founding fathers signed theirs
on the dotted line,

just put my John Doe in the box, please."

Novel Romance

I finally woke up this morning
and brushed my teeth
with Bailey's Irish Cream.

For breakfast, I cooked myself
a tale of lobster and filet mignon
with a chaser of mac 'n cheese.
I ate my feast in front of the roaring fire,
where I burned all the packets of low fat
oatmeal I could find,
and all the bills I owed.

I considered torching
my little black book of jerk's phone numbers,
but instead, used white-out. When it dried,
I took octopus ink to the wedding-dress
colored pages, and wrote
my first romance novel.

Then, just for fun, I called myself on the phone
and swore up and down I'd call back soon.
Then, I hung up, and speed dialed myself again,
to keep my promise,
and because I TRULY wanted to.

I kept that up all afternoon.

Eager to accomplish more,
I left a message on my boss's answering machine
saying I was just too love-sick to work,
anymore.

Noticing the late hour,
I got dressed in my finest
sequined evening gown
and glided out into the moonlit garden
where I waltzed with the wall flowers
and watered them with Evian
and pink champaign,
after tearing out the man-
icured hedges to make space for more wild
flowers my land lord mistakingly
calls weeds.

After such a productive day,
I retired to my boudoir
(I cannot even tell you of the romance
that ensued behind that door.)

But first,
I brushed my teeth.

Someone Might Get Burned

This poem is a double-edged serving knife:
dangerous. It cuts through frosted layers.
Taste the paper cut from licking shut
love letters (presumptuous french-kiss!) Return
address pressed on white after-thought of tree,
blood bitter as of yet; unsweetened chocolate bark.
I bake my pastries as I mix my words:
too impatient to let the butter melt,
two tablespoons of "Honey," clove and sage
for every one in print. My German oven
woos the heat in metrics, which I ignore.
Instead, I dance around the kitchen floor on fire
praying that my dough will rise in time.
A calculating muse urges me to send
more sweets to you, but someone might get burned.

Monsters Under The Covers

What place does "the shadow"
have in these pages?
Those quiet secrets
that fill your pill box,
or an abandoned shipping container somewhere
in a warehouse in Asia?
You know the ones
or maybe you've conveniently forgotten
what you buried in your backyard or the bottom
of the pond or your underwear
drawer?

If I were to serve
our darkest and bitter-most truths
would you gag and spew syllables
all over your white shirt or plead
for a few stanzas more?

Few drink their coffee black these days
other than addicts,
or connoisseurs.

When you can't sleep in the middle of the night

(too much caffeine) and you turn on the light
and my words scurry across your apartment floor,
will you stomp on them like the misunderstood
cockroaches that they are?

What scares me even more
is the thought that the monsters
who use to sleep under our beds in childhood
are now hiding under the covers
of this book.

This is why I am going to serve Grande
Lattes with whipping cream and vanilla sugar,
and the only insects on this platter
will be chocolate-covered:
rumor has it monsters are disarmed
by sweetness and caffeine.

That should keep you,
I mean, them,
satisfied for awhile.
Nudging them over with knees and elbows
only seems to make them want to snuggle closer.

So heed this warning if you yourself

should find yourself
tangled up in these cream-colored sheets:

there is no telling when, or if, or ever
they will go to sleep, or what might happen
in their dreams.

If you get frightened, screaming is always an option.
Or, you can turn your TV back on, real loud,
to drown out their growls
(that has worked for you before...?)

But remember, monsters are like cock roaches
and calories: just because you can't hear them,
doesn't mean they aren't there.
Instead, you might try disarming them,
-- even charming them --
with a mocha
or a kiss.
                    Which one do YOU prefer?

The Courage to Moan

An Angel moaned while hugging me.
Of course I wanted more. I wanted everything.

So, of course,
desire being dangerous to those with wings
(think moth to flame)
we acted real cool,
like strangers.

For a long time, I felt confused,
even betrayed,
as if the purrrrr of a cat,
or a mountain lion,
is a promise.
It's NOT!
Wildness falls into you like feathers
one moment
then rips you apart like claws on a pillow, the next.

This is nature.

I blamed the awkwardness on *his* fears,
his hesitations.

But, I was the stranger
to myself.

If only I had been ME enough;
"MEENOUGH!"

me with *courage;*
"MEWITHCOURAGE!"

I would have moaned *out loud*
while hugging him back.

What beautiful noises we could have made together!

"MMMMMMMMMMMMMMMMMMMMMMMMMMM
UUUUMMMOOOOMMMMMUUUUUUMMMMMM

MMMMMMMMMMMMMMMMMMMMMMMMMMMOO
OOOOOOOOOOOUUUUUUUUUUUUUUUUUMM
MMMMMMMMNNNNNNNNNNNOOOOOOOOOMM
MMMMMMOOOOOOOOOOOOOOAAAAAAAAAAA
AAAAAAAAAAAAAAAANNNNNNNNNNNNNNNN
NNNNNNNNNNNNNNNNNNNNNNNNNNNNNNN
NNNNNNNNNNMMMMMMMMMMMNNNNNNNN
NNNNNNNNMMMMMMMMMMMMMMMMMMN
NNNNNNNNNNNNN6N6N6NNNNNNNNNNNOOO
OOOOOOOOOOOOOOOOOOOOOOOOOOOOOOE
EEEEEEEEEEEEEEEEEEEEEEEEEEEEEEEEEEEEEEEEEEEE
EEEEEEEEEEEEEAAAAAAAAAAAAAAAAAWWWWWWW
WWWWWWWWWWWWWWWWWWWWWWWWWWWW
WWWWWWWWWWWWWWWWWWWWWMMMMM
MMMMOOOOOOOOOOOOOOOOORRRRRRRRRRR
RRRRRREEEEEEEEEEEEEEEEEEEEEEEEEEEEEEEEEEEEEE
DDDDDDDDDDDDDDDDDDOOOOOOOOOOOOOO
OOOOOOOOOTTTTTTTTTTTTTTTTTHHHHHHHHH
HHHHHHHHHHHHHAAAAAAAAAAAAAAAAAAAAAA
TTTTTTTTTTTAAAAAAAAAAAAAAAAAAGGGGGGGAAA
AAAAAAAAAAAAAAAAAIIIIIIIIIIIIIIIIIIIIIIIIIIIIIIIIIIIIIIIIII
IIIINNNNNNNNNNNNNNNNNNNNNNNNNNNNPPPP
PPPPPPPPPPLLLLLLLLLLLLLLLLLLLLLLLLLLLLLLLLEEE
EEEEEEEEEEEEEAAAAAAAAAAAAAAAAASSSSSSSSEEEEEM
MMMMMMMMMMMMOOORRRRRRRRRRRRRRRR
RRRRRRRRRRRRRRRRRRRRRRRRRRRREEEEEEEEEEE

Maalox Nights

My confused heart eats beats in squeezed tempos
strangling like the slimey mold-lipped sponge
the cleaning lady is too cheap to part with.

My bowels serve the tasteful social function
of a filthy sink. No one cares to know
how they grown and choke
syncopating the remains of artichokes
with devil's food moon cake and red curry
as pornographic pickles and the flank of steak
riff the plank to a gasterous sea
of heart-shards and soapy bile sharks.

While you were away (i was the one who left
but you were the one away, always away)
my fantasy threw a dinner party
at the moon, which only bruised it.

The guests were the "beautiful people"
sweetly rich and low with wit,
sporting gold plated balls and
zirconia studded boobs

while me and you sipped starlight out of a crystal
Doc Martin boot.

Even my fantasies are spiked with stomach bile
these madcap Maalox nights
Oh how i hate loving you.

Time is a Funny Thing

So you know someone for a lifetime:
a father, a god, a devil, a mother
that's suppose to be reason enough
to love one another.
Never mind that the fists of time may
blacken your eyes
batter your soul
stop the tickling of your heart's clock
by smashing it against the wall
as if "half-asleep" excuses such a silencing!

Time is a funny thing.
I have pried loose the many fingers
that clung to the ledge of my heart
claiming love.
Spiderman was a scammer,
a cat burglar,
and Mama always said, "Never
trust a man wearing web-weaving gloves."

I use to fashion myself a princess
believe-making in a slow conquer and come
"Climb the tresses of my treacherous locks

only *then* will your dirty paws be welcome!"

But time is a funny thing.
Two months ago I glimpsed you through your fame;
two weeks ago the trolls told me your true name;
two days ago we were slaying dragons high on acid
in each other's souls.

Today, I am dreaming up grim fairy tales
of enchanted forests and strung out heros,
of wizened owls, secret vows
and Hansel and Gretel
being shoved in an oven
and coming out whole
like gingerbread men.

Time is a funny thing
when we mix our metaphors into batter
and bake a delicacy of fishes and loaves
they turn into salmon-shaped breadcrumbs
leading us back to our origins
once upon a time
(and this poem,
which is merely a snack
on a park bench
along love's path)

and then even farther back
to the wicked stepmother's abode
-- the one who starved us.

We are always running away
to get back home.
The proverbial dog
chasing his fabled tail.
When he finally catches it,
will he feel satisfied,
wounded, or both?

Will he gobble himself up
until he disappears
like the cheshire cat?
How does that tale go, again?

Time is a funny thing,
to canines and felines,
and hungry witch-queens
who have the blood of ginger
on their wrinkled hands
and smell of chum.

That's why I am still laughing,
in spite of myself.

Weather the Storm

"Weather the storm!"
A curious expression.
It is a declaration or command
by the one who speaks it;
to the listener, a question.

Will I?
I will.
I will not die.
I will not dye my mood with your warpaint,
my mouth with your blow-up doll's lipstick,
my dignity with your rainbow of complaints.

Grey is the sky, my shade:
I exist somewhere between black and white.
A cloud is a cloud in its own right
it's not there only to highlight the blue
for the photographer's background.

I am cumulous.
I float. I rain
regardless of when your sun sets.

I am a Sunday newspaper
to be savored slowly
over a pot of morning
coffee

not a limerick scribbled
on the back of a twenty dollar bill
that flies out of the back seat of your BMW
when you are through reciting my ass.

Keep your red roses
and yellow excuses
out of my spectrum.

I am Chinese calligraphy,
not a child's finger painting.

Keep your thumbs
out of my plum pie.

"Weather the Storm," I say.
A curious expression.

I am the storm.
        You are the whether.

The Wrath of Peas
(Or, "Eat Your Peas, Dear")
For my father, who demonstrated his love
by trying to make us eat peas.

Alien.
Unmerciful.
Evil.
Martian-colored creature
you cannot fool me!
Sitting sooooo placidly on my plate,
trembling at the slightest sign of movement.
Squinty eyes taunt my fork,
mocking my fate.

I can predict the taste of your venomous,
much mashy-greenness;
I can feel
your wicked anticipation
for the oral invasion
that soon will come.

Your vegetable brothers
so sweet and straight
they are not of your kind.

I saw you winking your grassy eyes just now
shaking your hips when I sat at the table,
Don't think I am so easily seduced!

Yes, laugh all you want at my helplessness.
Others, bigger and brighter (ha!)
are under your propagandic power.
This is a shot gun wedding
and no one seems to care
that I left my heart in the mash potatoes.
Pea:
it seems it is be my duty,
my destiny
to eat you!

But, wait!
What is that under the table?
My hero?
My rescuer?
My garbage disposal?
That's a good doggie,
sit boy, sit!
Open your mouth
and eat my peas,
Dear!

My love is Mormon

My love is Mormon

but my lust
is a liberal
Jew.

This Morning Sickness

This morning
I am so sick with lust
I think I might throw up.
Won't someone prescribe
an Ayurvedic cure?

Never mind.
I would drink the whole bottle,
and end up right back
at the naturopaths' office
where all this started,

in love with the doctors
who gave me a taste
of my own medicine.

Cacophony of Toads

Tadpoles are skinny-dipping in my soul,
growing into horny toads who'll leap out
one day and splash into your golden pond.
The realization of your love, your touch
after this eternity... I tremble green and croak.
How I long to be torn apart; quartered
by your four horses galloping in each direction.
All that will be left is One heart beating. It will
beat so loud they will hear it on every continent:
children will recognize the sound of God breathing;
lovers will snake & moan, undulating to the rhythm;
madmen, murderers and saints will laugh,
entranced, and fall to their knees, weeping.
The world will hold hands and dance in my blood.

Part II: Eat Prey, Love

Some outlaws lived by the side of the lake
The minister's daughter's in love with the snake
Who lives in a well by the side of the road
Wake up, girl! We're almost home

We should see the gates by mornin'
We should be inside by evening,

sun sun sun
burn burn burn
MOON, MOON, MOON
i will get you
soon,
soon,
soon

i am the lizard king
i can do anything

Jim Morrison, *Celebration of the Lizard*

Bruised Apples

It isn't true
that "Time heals wounds."
Healing implies a closing, a leaving,
a once broken-winged sparrow now flying away;
human beings have ten toes and mortal hearts
which root us to the ground.
We are really trees that grow rings around
the other circles of our days.

Nothing goes away.
Scabs thicken into scars that serve as war paint,
good for keeping settlers an arrow's length away.

I wasn't a warrior then, but green apprentice
to a shaman. You were that and I a sapling
in the glen tossing leaves on you
that you would chew and spit
onto your other-woman's open sores:
a salve like Adder's Tongue
(an antivenin when the fresh leaves bruise)
but also poison Snakeweed.
This I fed to you, and the mother of your child.

Yet every other weak

you came back to kneed
my aching roots deeper into soil
and once you watered me with tears and cried,
"I share my core with you!"
These were the only tears you shed out-loud
in our ten years, a cherished offering.

Now I wonder what my mine were worth
and are...

so many bushels full.

So much of the harvest feels like despair:
hard, heavy, square hours of grandfather clocks
leaning on our migrant backs.
But the minute hand surpasses the hour
as the turtle passes the hare
and we're reminded to keep facing forward
if we want to win the race
even though the starting line
and the finishing line
are the same.

Once,
we crawled into a second,
wrapped around each other Indian-style

no beginning and no end
to our eyes, mouths and other
musky wounds: we were curved into completion
in a seeded womb.

Moments like these are shaped like apples:
sweet and light and round;
they can be juggled, polished, swallowed,
collected in woven baskets
by fearless, loving hands.

It isn't true that time heals.
God gave our bodies openings
not meant to close.

Perhaps it is the wounds
that heal time;
the bruises
that make the apple seeds spill forth
and grow.

Roar of Finch

I wanted him to hear the wild bird
fluttering in the center of my being,
that yellow finch
who chirped a lion's roar.

Perhaps her tiny wings could stir up dust
one speck which might reflect all he wished to know
about himself (which is to say, all she
ever wished to know of fear and love.)

I sent him an e-mail and attached a pair of pliers
to tear apart the giant, bamboo cage
so big no chinese man would dare to air it
in the park on Sunday morn
or balance it on the dashboard of his bus for luck.

In reply
He didn't.

Just shoved a mirror through cyberspace,
which flew into the "O" of my mouth
and scurried down the "U" of my throat --
(Love letters have a way of boomeranging.)

I gagged, then screamed,
then stuck a shotgun
deep into my esophagus with trigger pulled.
I was only trying to shoot
the embarrassment of ignorance
and felt - shame of self
revelation into oblivion.
Instead,
I shot the looking-glass
that hologram
which shattered into a billion tiny shards,
each projecting that which was not real
and my own face.
Only then did I surrender to my shame
and something more, yet unnamed
and sit with both
in silence.

Moments passed,
then lifetimes
as I searched the cracks and empty spaces
praying for a glimpse of golden feathers,
or a tiny arrow-footprint in the sand
pointing toward my own future
gravesite
where I might re-coup

or resurrect.

When I arrived home
I leaned up against the cold stone
of my aloneness
and noticed
what had at first appeared as darkness
was the dark-brown, molted mantle
of an adolescent eagle.
She was feeding
on the dying, yellow songbird.

I watched in horror
as she tore flesh with beak and talon,
devouring, disemboweling,
dismembering me in nature's callous way.

But my eyes began to adjust to the darkness
seeing emerged from seeming
and I saw that with every bloody swallow
my rapt-eyed raptor grew
in soul and wing.

Now, with a sigh and a shudder,
I settle deep inside her belly
feeling the echos of a finch's chirp

harmonize with the eagle's scream.

I hope that soon my time will come to fly again
but not until I digest this darkness
and learn to dance with the shadow
fluttering and roaring
in the circle
of my being.

The Lizard Thieves

We are born thieves.
The winged, the scaled, the porous fleshed,
the amoeba and the whale:
all life starving and obsessed.
We are all consumed with consuming
one another
like the Earth consummates her self.

Perhaps that's why we come alive
imprisoned in our mother's womb.
We are unfledged jailbirds,
incarcerated in the holding cells of another's body.
Even here we tap and guzzle blood
like the children suckling stolen beer
in the parking lot of Seven Eleven,
the first sacred rites of shop lifting.

When the interrogator with the harsh light
and latex gloves slaps us on the delivery
table,
we awaken to ourselves in solitary
confinement of our own skin.
We learn to do hard time locked up
in the flesh of paradox:

vowing in every breath to rehabilitate
even as we plot the Great Escape.

In turn, we learn to turn,
crawl, walk, dig our heels in, or flee
in desperation through tunnels
that empty out into the desert
where we will wander for forty days, or forty years,
in search of salvation by whispering
to reptiles and falling
to our knees to pray, or fornicate.

When we come at last
home, late to the final supper,
Lust is served on a silver platter
with an apple in his mouth.

(If you don't know what I am talking about,
go ask Eve, the knowledgable diva in the red lipstick.
Don't bother with Adam: he'll deny it all.)

As born-agains,
our smiles and supplicating hands
are the first parts of us to resurrect:
we learn to pick-pocket forbidden things
we launder in our toothless mouths.

By the time we are old enough
to grow a villain's mustache
and cause the damsel adequate distress,
we are adepts at the art of theft
(and the craft of self flagellation.)
We steal shy glances
at the those whose beauty entrances us,
only to conspire with Eros to cast Psyche
out of Mt. Olympus,
for ripping off
our masks.

How easily we cat-burglar
blue flecked eggs from mysterious nests,
and fossils found in history's caves;
the answers to unspoken questions,
innocence,
patience,
and Rumpelstiltskin's
name.

We plunder the power
of the wind, sun and sea
the treasures of what we are
and what we are longing
to become:

the gossamer wings of dragon flies,
sage,
berries dripping juicily from the vine,
shells the shape of sacred geometry,
and oysters
hinting at the possibility
of pricelessness.

Our whole lives we kidnap each other:
baby blue jays fallen from the nest, needing rescue;
rattled snakes, croaking frogs
and lizards hypnotized and stunned
by altered states of consciousness.
The ransom is wild bliss,
to be delivered in unmarked bills
of swans, or raptors.

We are all owls yearning
to steal the lizard's last breath:
the Eternal Kiss.
We are all iguanas,
pursing our lips.

And in the end,
when the Great Fireman comes
to extinguish the last embers of desire and dearth,

and the Warden hands us our own skeleton's
key and our one true belonging
confiscated at the intake;
there will be only two things left to steal:

A pair of angel wings
and a tube of blood
red lip stick.

A Man's House

You, a tower of steel
a house made of rebar
no big bad she-wolf
could ever blow
down.

Master of the House
so self-contained
don't you know
there are more earth-friendly shelters?
The caves between words
the breaths between moans
the smooth places between the thorns
of the rose where the butterfly alights.
Your house of cards
will come fluttering
down
even if you super-glue it, cement it, weld it together
it will fall or disintegrate
on singed wings.

Vulnerability!
How I wish I could buy a man's tears

by the cup or the pint,
or just enough to fill my amber perfume bottle.
Do you think they sell them on Ebay?
I would click "buy now" and not even haggle.

When a man begins to weep
hard seed blossoms into lily;
clover fields return to green;
glacier ice melts into trout streams from which the deer
and the elk and mysterious others drink.
When a man wades into these deep waters,
thunderclaps give way to the love songs of thrushes
and sunlight warms the willow's skin.
It doesn't hurt to hold you anymore.

You, a subfloor of steel
a fort of reinforced concrete
a lion tangled up in barbed-wired thorns.
If you pretend
to have no wounds
how can we lick them?
Bleed,
so we know where to kiss away the pain.
Bleed, for blood is our birth rite too!
Together, our wounds form our storm shelter,
our wine cellar, our well.

No.
I don't need a man of steel.
That's what my Smith and Wesson M&P,
fireplace poker, Ginsu knife, and vibrator are for.

I need a man of bamboo
who can bend to my hurricanes.

I need quivering aspen:
deciduous trees in love with *every* season.

Won't you be paper birch,
whose pliancy is its strength?
It can be written on, woven into
poems, baskets and canoes.

When you need to be mighty,
be Black Birch: its phloem is medicine.

Be a tree house; a jungle refuge
for spider monkeys and jaguars,
for pigmy marmosets and those
impossibly green and minuscule frogs
only those National Geographic photographers
in the Amazon capture.

Then I can hang my swing in your tallest branches
and we can fly together.

And when you grow sad or stormy,
as all men and cloud forests do
from time to time,
my canopy will have grown close enough
to help shelter yours.

This house
will be stronger
than any
steel.

Mermaid and the Mariner

They went on a date
That wasn't really a date
but wasn't really not a date
to the maritime museum.

He talked about his love for the sea and ancient
schooners.
She told him boats made her think of shipwrecks and
death,
and victims abandoned on deserted islands.
This depressed her.

They walked around looking at displays and yellowed
photographs of captains and their catches.
He invited her to lunch, his treat, at the expensive
restaurant on the harbor:
"They serve the lobster with garlic butter,
and the fried squid is to die for."

She thought of the cruelty of dropping
living creatures into boiling water,
and how he might assume it could never work between
them, and dump her,

if he knew she was a vegetarian.

How nervous she'd be eating in front of him
thinking thoughts of him being a clam,
or baby shrimp killer
and not knowing if he might try to kiss her afterward
which she'd like, if he really wasn't gay,
which he still seemed like he might be
because he had complimented her color coordination,
but not her (an important distinction)
and told a story about a dog that tracked mud onto his
white carpet.
She was sure straight men did not have white carpets,
and if they did, they would not be anal
about dirty dog feet.

She thought, "I can never bring him to my home,
which is dusty and small with pink pillows
and every inch of the space taken with my stuff."

Where would he ever put his things if the ice were
broken and they moved in together?

"Thanks, but I'm not hungry," she lied, feeling her own
coldness inside.

She had wondered, in her head, why he never told her
anything about his other work or his personal life.
She contemplated if he were celibate, or married,
or a perv.
But now, he spoke of an ex-wife, and his last girlfriend
and her golden retriever,
whom he still had joint custody of
and took on long walks along the shore.
She silently questioned why he was telling her all this,
and if I he wasn't inappropriately self-disclosing?

He brought up the names of Ruth, and Sue and Nina,
common acquaintances they worked with
and respected. She felt jealous,
and analyzed if he secretly wished
he could be with them, and why he said nice things
about these other women, but hadn't noticed she spent
two hours that morning
curling her hair.

He made a joke, and rubbed shoulders with her,
but feeling sorry for herself, she flinched,
and side stepped him.
He walked her to her car, in awkward silence,
until he closed with,
"Enjoy the rest of your day."

He did not traverse
the great distance between them
to hug her
like he had after happy hour the Friday before.
"Thanks, you too." She said politely, then drove away,
forever.

When he didn't call her again,
she was devastated.

The Terror and Seduction of Art

A Poem made a pass at you; her chaos
mountainous, you ordered her out.
A Masterpiece wooed you into rendezvous;
his hues dangerously wild, his brush strokes
too bold, you ran back to Paint-By-Numbers.
Invited to a dinner dance by a Tango,
feet rarely felt floor, yet presence caressed presence,
"How do I trust this?" You ripped the soles
from your shoes. When Regret was the only suitor
left, a fail-safe, familiar provider,
you accepted this cold hand in marriage,
gave birth to Bitterness, and retired.
Of late, a Love Song tosses stones at your window.
When longing hurts more than fear, you will open.

This Kind of Love

Why is it wrong to love
those who won't love us back?

In exchange for watering her
does the rose have to give us anything
other than her beauty and her scent
(as if there is anything more we could want than that?)

Why can't I love what I love
and just have it be simply that:
my own heart blossoming pink
petals velvet silk as a baby's cheek
that everyone wants to rub
their noses up against
and kiss
and drink as honey bees sip ambrosia?

Sweetness does not expect much from the bee
other than to carry her fluidity into future fields
of green and rose and lavender
where children dance and lovers
find each other again.
What is wrong with *this* kind of love?

The Threshold

This poem
is not a poem.

This is a doorway
that leads

from one room
to another.

I am one room.

You are the other:

A kitchen with mixing bowls
full of dough for kneading;
hard-crusted bread
full of cinnamon and secrets,
sweet butter and bitter
sunflower seeds
I wish could explode into the wet soil
of my garden.

There is a stove for simmering,

cupboards for holding,
chairs in four directions for roundtable discussions,
card playing, arm wrestling, thanksgiving offerings.

The other room
was built for dreaming.

There is a closet full of
skeletons and silk sorrys
furry animal slippers,
sequined gowns with price tags faded
but still attached
worn long ago at fancy balls thrown by
fancy ghosts
that bounce and echo
on the dance floor of a poets'
lonely imagination.

Here there is a chair by the window
strewn with moonlight and lovers' clothing
peeled off and cast away
like the hard, protective skin of forbidden fruit
by the mouths and hands of
the starving
desperate to consume
expose

know and be known
salvation and damnation
sprouting
from the same seed.

There is a bed
(the blood-red sheet tangled
in itself)
the crime scene
of countless dream-time murders
and miracles:
flying on magic carpets
floating towards the ceiling
roaming foreign cities
an endless procession of wild
animals, dark men and monsters
trying to break in
succeeding

as the plane is missed
the lines forgotten
the mirrors' reflection fallen into
as teeth and hair fall out
falling down stairs
falling below the surface of
corpse-infested waters

saving drowning children
nursing dolphins
escaping sharks
landing on safe islands
where the fruit is sweet
and shaped like mandalas.

This poem
is not a poem.

This is a doorway
that leads
from one room
to another.

I am one room.
You are the other.

When the gathering of daylight comes
these rooms can glimpse into
each other
but they can only ever touch
at the archway
where they say hello and goodbye
at the same time every moment

sublimely never knowing
what it is to make a home together
in the other's middle.

Together, we are a threshold

Summer Into Fall

There is a willow tree in the wood
down by the witch's stream,
protected by hummingbirds.

If I were to take your hand
and lead you there
two children
searching the dappled sunlight
for a lighter shade of green
where the waters leap over rock
like pipers and toads and bouncing hares
would you lean on me?
Back to front
as I lean upon the thick and ancient trunk
and let my restless hands come to rest
on your bare knees
two butterflies
weary from fluttering from the flower of want
to the flower of need
yet still elated to be alive.

In this sacred space
of Earth and dragonfly

could I nestle down
a deer sinking into deep moss,
a pregnant lark wiggling into downy nest,
and press my lips to your hair
and kiss the hollow of you neck?

Would this feel safe,
or dangerous?
Under the voyeuristic eyes of robber Jays
who gossip righteously about what is to come
as if the future had already passed
as if the summer had stolen into fall
and our children, named Memories Of What Is
and Was
had flown South to winter separately,
grown and gone.

There is a weeping willow in the grove
down by a warlock's pond,
guarded by ravens.
Take me, there.

Two old souls searching the sunlit dapples
for the deeper shades of green,
still leaning,
but children no longer.

Undreamt

I want to write a poem
using words that have never been written.

I want to hold a song to my lips
and kiss it with a passion
that has never been expressed.

I long to be things
no one has ever been,
in wild places, yet undreamt.

But, as the Science-fiction writer knows --
the one who accidentally predicts
fifty-years in advance
the advances of his nation --
The future has already been written.

This poem, unfinished,
is already relic;
this page: a crypt.
Each word perfectly preserved
like King Tutankhamen
in the reader's ear.

The reader is already museum;
mausoleum.

And I, just being born,
am long ago
dead.

Questing for a Moment

What if this is all there is?

That pulse in your wrist.
That pen on the table.
That glass of moonlight on the sill.
That knife glistening on the counter.
That checkbook waiting in the drawer.
That still-born child in the grave.
That question, that inhale, this sigh?
What if this is your entire existence:
what is. No meaning
other than what you write
or suckle or sip or kill or spend or ask or
breath now, then and what will ever be –
all wrapped up in one, single, moment:

this moment.

What if this hard bed that you lie on
and the slow-breathing darkness
that sleeps softly on top of you
like a child or lover lulled into oceanic slumber
by the monotonous ebb and flow of your heart tide;

what if this surface and this darkness
touch to form the only cocoon
that will ever harbor you and
you, the grub, the monarch butterfly
are all one, now,
complete in your perfect imperfection.
Chrysalis as it has always been.
Chrysalis as it will always be.

What if you are the only Self
you will ever be?
You: the sail, the wave, the rudder, the wind: one
boat. One sea.
One soul anchored
to the cold depths of a moment
that place so far from sunlight
even the shadow is dead.

This is the only place
where you have the fearlessness to ask,
"What if this is All there is?"
And to accept that answer
infinitely.

My Inner Poet and Our (Ex) Husband

My inner poet watches the night sky and
waits.
She is a wispy waif, with sun-licked hair
and sea-breathed feathers; she tucks her wings
into the back of her parachute pants and laughs,
intoxicated with air-juice.
She hangs out with infamous stars
and that ham in the moon.

My inner poet is a voice. That light.
She thrives on blueberry-buckle baby food
(not nonpareils, the favorite candy
of my "Inner Film Critic.")

My inner poet sleeps on the green moss of large rocks
that look like giant tortuous shells.
Every now and then they move,
so when she wakes, she doesn't know where she is
which suits her just fine.

When she gets chilled, she dives
into any waterbed she can find;
her choice of indoor furniture.

Recently my inner poet took a shower in the basement
of our husband's boyhood home.
Standing in a small, tin washtub, no curtain,
under a make-shift spout,
the air was bitingly cool, the water soothingly hot.
To have such space...Ahhh!
"Elbows should be entirely free when one is
shampooing their hair," she coos.

There was a clothesline down there,
and an ancient Maytag washing machine
she would have liked to see in use
(as long as someone else was using it.
She doesn't like to clean,
but for meditative purposes.)

My inner poet is a contemplative
bird. Not a duck or a swan,
but a fey pterodactyl
who loves to bathe in pre-historic baths.
Once she showered among aggressive mint leaves
and snaking vines at the Loflorian Nature Sanctuary
during a Witches' Ball the very last weekend of a warm
October somewhere in Southern Indiana.
Stark naked in the seductive sunshine and scandalized
trees, she waved to the greenery and to a smiling soul

who happened to be passing by.
It was O.K. He was naked too,
long beard hanging loose over a bulging belly
(he did have on hiking boots.)
My inner poet admired his courage to roam with all
flesh kissing the breeze,
while I wondered if he'd get bug bites in places we
wouldn't care to scratch.

My inner poet scratches her head sometimes,
telling all those thoughts to calm down and go to sleep
so she can go to dream: she works the graveyard shift.
Maybe my scalp is just dry from all those showers...
I think it calms her, like warm milk, making love,
and getting lost in wild places where she finds herself.

Getting lost was how we met our husband on Hooker
Hill in Itaewon, South Korea, after Jewish synagogue
services. Fate, and some Swedish businessmen
lead us to him in a country-western bar
called the "Grand Ole Opry,"
where his inner poet was two-stepping poetry.
His feet sang in metered verse, rhyming cowboy twangs
of love and pain, gain and loss, lonely soldiers and wild
English teachers as his hips spelled out
suggestive metaphors.

Turning Truths around the dance floor gave him the
courage to look into my eyes.

My husband's poet wears binoculars.
Pumpkin pies tremble at the sight of him. Lovingly
he calls me "Goober" and "Dork."
I hurl Yiddish curse words back at him, "Smeckel!"
"Kish Mein Touchess!"
There are some things which should not be understood.

Last July our poets honeymooned for five mariachi days
on the tequila shores of Mexico;
every afternoon we made love to the beat of the
glorious sun. Unlikewise, I spent most of Chicago
poeting alone: my relatives, stress and subzero
temperatures disconcert him.
Now and then we play a game of "Hide and Seek."
My inner poet would like to change this game to
"Seek and Find."

When my husband's inner poet gets lost,
he just gets confused.
"Why do you cry when we make love?" he demands,
"And for heaven's sake, why do you laugh!"
He forgets that tears are the sound of my inner poet's
deepest breathing, and laughter is her heart beating

"I am the sky."
Why do most men only understand when our
OUTER poets makes noise?
Often now when we're together,
I miss him.

My inner poet watches the night sky
and waits for the re-turning.
She tries to see everything she is meant to see,
but she only has *inner* seeing: feeling.
She can dance point on the high beam of a rainbow
but stumbles off street curbs, walks into walls
de-programs computers, sets off alarm systems,
and rebels against the shutting off of lights:
night lights, day lights, headlights, heart lights,
de-lights, and spotlights.
This makes her irritating,
or endearing,
depending on who's doing the writing.

When my Inner Poet writes,
my heart stops
bleeding.

Lotus Wounds

I thought that human hearts
hardened from too much hurting
scarred from too much scaring;
that the knife blade of rejection and recrimination,
of doors flung wide open then slammed shut
on the fingers of longing
would cut me down or cause eternal bleeding.

So why is this bludgeoned heart blooming
like a cactus flower in high desert springtime?

Is a giant's reservoir of tears pouring
enough to nourish back a life
cut down to her aching roots
driven to her beanstalk knees
prostrated in broken pose lower than despair
or shame fiercer than a wounded lion's roaring?

Perhaps tears must merge with consciousness --
"Human photosynthesis" if our souls are ever to grow
into the promise of wholeness and embodied dreams?

How else could this devoured orb be opening

like a red lotus blossom blooming
like the swollen earth-entrance
to a lover's secret longing
earth and sky exploding
as she dances sacred Sun Dance
four days and nights in the circle
of her lover
lusting more insatiably
than Coyote for Harvest Moon
half crazed from mortal hunger
feeding only on her lover's rain,
lips, wounds, groins groaning
into the mechanisms of an ancient loom
weaving wings together
light enough to fly to God, to bliss
losing self to find One Self
hurting to hunt healing
east eating west
two lovers on the same solo
of an endless vision quest.

I have learned that four hands drive the stake
into the initiate's ventricles,
never only two (unless they're your own)
and it isn't blood alone that pours
but blood mixed with love

red mixing with the white of doves
fluttering down ribs and thighs
screaming mixed with humming
merging into sounds of deep, black water
as we swim backward into oceanic cocoon.

The knife was my knife
forged by my own self-hatred and redemption
placed in the hands of skilled surgeons
who pried open the red door of me
and found God waiting in side.

God greeted them
like he greeted you
the moment you were born:
the doctor slapped God
the baby breathed in
together
we sigh out loud.

This was the first cruel act of human kindness
the Genesis of unconditional love
the alchemy of hearts opening
holy.

To Get Carried Away or Clean

I am looking at your toes right now
resting on the edge of our coffee table.
They are covered with beach sand
and I'm not sure if I should scold you
or become a hermit crab
and nibble on them anyway
and make my way
up your musseled rocks
until we both get carried away
by the salty rush
of your tidal waves,
or if I should just get the vacuum out
and beach comb
the dining room rug.

Reflection on Drowning
in the Throes of a Poem

Narcissus
must
have
been

a

p
o
e
t
.

Part III: The Violence of Feathers

"These violent delights have violent ends
And in their triumph die, like fire and powder,
Which as they kiss consume."

- William Shakespeare, *Romeo and Juliet*

My Love is a Bristlecone Pine Forest

My love is an ancient
bristlecone forest
drenched in the honey-milk of the Moon.
Here, even the shadows become kittens
lapping at the sweetness streaming
from the breast of the lunar Goddess
down onto the wind-swept cradle
of the white mountains.

The wrinkled nursemaids
disguised as four thousand year-old trees
bend to twisted knee
and pine.

When the Moon's consort, Scorpius,
finally appears
(so late that even those with no concern for time
take notice)
these gnarled grandmothers grumble and fret
"Look at how he claws and pinches
under her long black cape!
He's always leaving trails of bruised
stars in his wake!"

It's true,
his embraces sting
and his secrets are legendary.
But then again, so are hers.

When he moves close to her celestial body
how she shines! how she flames!

When he scuttles off to other horizons
she wanes and broods.
When her hopes become eclipsed long enough,
the crocuses and morning glories
fear suicide.

Yet, she knows all too well the nature
of complex constellations, and muses.
There is no one to forgive, but herself.

When she forgives, she is full.

At the edge of the grove
a murder of crows
watch over the ardent evergreens
those primordial predecessors
whom will live as long into the whims of the future
as they grew from the soiled will of the past.

The winged ones feel jealous and wise
as they gawk at the supplicating crones
who even in this late hour
are standing on their heads
spreading their heavy and scarred legs skyward,
spreading themselves so wide open
with earthly desire
that sparrows nest
between their creaking thighs.

These the black birds will hunt
when the King of Fire rises
and the Queen of Water retreats
to her underworld quarters
turning a blind eye
to the violence of feathers.

Fire and Powder

We were standing
in my mother's heated foyer.
The harsh light above us warning.
The door to the closet gawking.
The coats lined up front to back like soldiers.
The window panes frosted over, obscuring
the cold reality
just beyond our court yard.

All week, and
all those long and lovely and devastatingly lonely
months and years,
I had been waiting,
waiting to tell you how deeply I loved you;
waiting to vow heroically,
"I would even *die* for you!"
It was true, then and even now.
How young Shakespeare must have been
when he imagined Romeo! And so was I.

But, I was also female and shy
and gagged by the taboo
of speaking truth.

So instead, I set about to engrave our love story
on the nape of your neck
with the ink and chisel of my lips
in the iambic pentameter of vampires.

You did not come
alive, as usual.
You staggered away
as if I was murdering you.

And so I was.
A voice from beyond the grave
rose from the hades of your throat:

"Sometimes, after leaving you, I take
a dagger to my own neck and draw
blood over the blush of roses you planted.
I try to make your mark look like a shaving cut
so 'She' won't suspect, or accuse"

You turned a darker shade of agony,
then, something worse:

"Some nights, after making love with you,
I go home in the early hours,
take a shower, and when she reaches for me

have to satisfy her.
Do you know how that
-- how this --
is destroying me?"

Somewhere far off in the distance
a glacier calved into the ocean.
The coats turned up their collars and shivered.
The roses wilted.
Romeo and Juliet died
all over again.

Cracked Angels

It is hard to swallow
after morning prayers
we contemplate our bacon:
pigs walk and play and procreate
please repeat your arguments for eating meat
I'll chew them over when I get to work.

At work
the children have no arms or legs
that work.
No voices to produce words.
Only unprofitable grunts
brays, moans, croaks;
dissertations of the soul
so unmarketable
Kevorkian minds
and Nazi kinds
would chop these "children of the useless limbs"
willow trees that reach ad nauseam
but never touch.

Yet they do!
They hit us so hard
their own mothers sentence them

here to life imprisonment
(hard labor, hard time)
in the name of good. God,

should we saw them down?
Babies with fingers that petrify like wood;
gnarled fists I wish could be shaken at the world
instead of stuffed into monstrous splints
so their hands will grow wide open
exposed like virgins on their backs
knees spread, bedsores on thigh,

"Sorry my coffee break ran over
so I couldn't turn her over on time.
At least she didn't die."

I clutch sweet Ava in my arms,
one three year old who weighs ten pounds.
This blessed protégé
is more gifted than the rest:
though paralyzed from the neck down
she can smile.

This cracked angel
with lips for wings
eats ambrosia through a tube.

The hands of strangers wash her
change her
someday a "caregiver" could rape her
like those stories one hears
of lonely shepherds and their animals.

"The Lord is
my shepherd I shall not want."

I pray she grows ugly with age.

Prayer To Tsunami

Tsunami, you were hungry!

Did appetizer of a billion bones appease?
If only we had made sacrifice to you sooner:
a sacred fish, or burnt herbs, wrapped in prayer,
smoked with drumbeats, filleted with rattles,
served at Neptune's feet...

would this have swayed you
from your kicking tantrum?

Some splash you made over a million asian rooftops
and a thousand tourist bikinis.
Your cry was enough to wake
the whole world;
your tears the second coming
of Noah's flood. Our grief is your ark.

You ordered your main course young, like veal.
Uncountable children's bodies
broken like twigs in our daily genocide of trees;
broken like the still-warm bodies of baby birds
shot down from countless nests
with countless bullets.

Eat them, Tsunami, Eat them!
Don't say this was only sport, or vengeance.
You *must* be a subsistence hunter, after all.
Drink their blood and swallow their flesh,
bring nourishment and strength
to the unbreakable chains of life.

Let us touch them again as we bury ourselves
in the white sands
that are sifted with bits of their bones,
sands that shelter hermit crabs and eggs
soon to hatch 100,000 turtles
who will run in one
giant tsunami
towards their destiny.

With each fish we eat
let us swallow the children you swallowed.
Let us sprinkle their memory from every salt shaker,
sip their essence from each glass of water and wine.
When we dream of swimming, or drowning,
let those whirling pools or dank swamps
be the souls you consumed
consuming us.

Tsunami, Oh Tsunami,

Never again will we speak your name in vain.
Eat! Eat! Your plate is full of humanity!

But please!
Save no room
for dessert.

Minefield of Roses

I watched a rose grow in a minefield
in Bosnia-Herzegovina.

I drank cappuccino under a rose-colored sunset
in Tuzla's old city square,
where 74 young people were slaughtered.

I listened to my sweet friend Leyla,
a 19 year old Muslim nurse,
who smelled of roses in sunshine
as she sipped whipped cream and justified
the revenge killings of Serbs;
neighbors who drank together.

"What you would do if they your house burned,
or murdered your family? If there were no court or
police to justice serve?"

It is difficult to understand the dialectics of war.
What are we when we can understand?
This is all I'll confess to having learned:

Fertilized ground will nourish seeds or bombs.

Gourmet coffee grounds end up like corpses,
rotting in the ground.

What goes around comes around and what comes
around, goes.

Don't smell the roses too closely.

The Sunken Elders

Grandfather, Grandmother,
where have you gone?
We are snails without shells.

Abalone glistens in the sun
yet what absent shapes it makes in the dark.

Once, when I was diving
off the coast of Dominique
I found a trap 30 feet under the current.

Inside of it was something floating:
a decaying conch shell or coconut,
but also a rotting head
buried in the sand by his own body, long ago.

The tide,
angry at what tries to hide,
dragged it out to sea.
The head, having lived its entire life behind bars
on doors, blinds on windows,
fences around private property
and walls around cities

sought out the familiar,
as heads are want to do.

This underwater cage
surely abandoned by crab hunters
during hurricane season
opened its door like Howard Johnson's.
Naturally, the head moved right in.
(It's hard to pass up a free continental breakfast, social
security, and a senior discount.)

This is the grave where our elders live.

And why we are now cheerless guppies and sea worms

Instead of starfish
And orca whales.

The Test

We were sitting on the couch
when I asked him if he wanted to read the love sonnet
I had just taken three days and nights
to compose. Irritated at being distracted from TV
and eBay and at my unpublished fantasies
he muttered, "When your book comes out,
I'll read it."

Sometimes I don't know
if he is being sarcastic and resentful
that my life has become a poem
while his remains remote-controlled
or motivational
to help my profession become something others
will actually buy and swallow
like pulp
fiction on the New York Times Best Seller List
or orange juice.

We've been dreaming
that I will become rich
so he can swim
in his own inner wealth.
I scribbled poetry all over that real estate contract

long ago, making it null and void.
But he still hangs out on that old pier,
starring into the nihilism of a soulless job
and avoiding the subject of change
unless its me who's jangling it in my pocket.
He's fishing for salvation in a dried up pond
and I fear if he doesn't catch a swordfish soon
in the depths of his own ocean,
or pull excalibur from the stone in his own shoe
and stomp on a few cyclops or dragons
he'll throw me back into the same sea
from which I, Calypso, came and
bury himself
in some other siren.

To avoid this epic nightmare
I am staying away from the beach for awhile
and buying him planks of tiger wood at Home Depot
so he can become a wild animal
or fashion himself a knight's staff
or a magic wand.

We all need a legend.

And maybe just maybe
he can make a fortune on eBay

so I can retire.

He's going to roar
when he reads this poem, like King Richard
the Lionhearted roared on the battlefield,
or King Henry the 8th roared in the bedroom
and have me beheaded.
Or maybe, he will meow like a kitten,
and thank me, his jester
for courting the artist within him,
the one locked in a box
of watercolors.

Sometimes he doesn't know
if I'm being sarcastic and resentful,
or motivational,
and neither does my editor.

But I have learned not to underestimate him.
He wouldn't attend the workshop on sacred love
held in our living room last week
but during the break
when I walked through the bedroom,
I found him reading the Karma Sutra.

His understanding of the human condition is profound,

and I forget, often,
that spirituality takes many forms:
even the discipline of time cards
and putting up with difficult bosses
and girlfriends high on metaphors.
Sometimes even more than tarot cards
or writing poems.

At least by the time he reads this
it will be safely harbored in hardcover,
and we'll both take solace
in the fact that one person, at least
bought my book.
(Yes, I am making him pay.)

If he shows no reaction
I'll know he lied when he promised to read it
cover to cover,
or he read the other sutras
and reached enlightenment
slightly
before I did.

My Hot Spud

You ask me if I still love you
after all these years and I see a potato
with its many eyes and earth smell

and I'm not sure if it us rotting
after all these years
or still delicious
baked twice with cheddar and sour cream
and bacon-bits that I pretend aren't there
because they aren't kosher.

Once, I asked you if you wanted to play
"Hot Potato"
and you threw a burning spud at me and I dropped it,
screaming,

"How could you do that to me
after all these years!?"
and you said, confused,
"But you said let's play Hot Potato."

After all these years, I have learned I get
what I ask for
and how to make mashed potatoes.

You ask me a second time,
"Do you still love me?"
thinking I am ignoring the question.
Your expression is sour
cream.

I smile and say,
"Does a potato love salt?"

Please save the rest of your silly questions
for Mrs. Potato Head.

The Moon's Arc

Last night,
under a Darth Vader sky
I mourned you   and
and
cried   cried
        and   and
            cried   cried
                    and   cried   and

cried
until the islanders begged me to stop
for fear of rising sea levels;
until Neptune jabbed me in the side
with his fishing spear and called to the moon,
"Put on your rubber boots and get out here
to mop up the tide!"

The moon gave her tyrannical lover a dangerous look,
then whispered to me
in a voice only surrenderers can hear:
"There is an ark waiting
at the source
of your tears."

I closed my damp eyes
and sailed backward
until I came home.

The door opened
I greeted myself.
First, I took off soggy shirt and shoes.
Then, I made a cup of reality,
watered the plants,
ate humble pie,
inspected the wrinkles of my mirror,

watched the news,
fell
asleep and dreamt that I was a desert
and you were a camel leading nomadic tribes
to freedom across my dunes;
that I was prehistoric sky
and you a pterodactyl
hunting to feed your hungry children
as I lifted you unimaginably
high on my currents.

I woke up
thirsty, hot,
full and
noticed strange feathers
strewn about the room.

The room became a boat
that sailed out the door.
The street was still a river of tears
but it had given rise to leaping dolphins
and mermaids pulling themselves up on street curbs
waiting for legs to sprout.
Fishermen excitedly cast their nets
Into deep shadows.

The sun tipped his hat at me
as I floated by on a bed of diamonds
and I smiled back,
noticing what had been there all along but
had been taken for mirage:

All God's children were playing together
on one wondrous shoreline
of grief.

Transgression

You told me once, long ago,
before one can confront, one must love.
Maybe that is why you plucked the feathers
from a dove and pinned the wings of a butterfly
to the wall:
to keep us from speaking
unutterable truths.

You shamed me for loving you.

No, that's not right. Not right at all. I shamed myself.

You shamed me for what I might do, if I ever stopped.

The desire is to be known, completely.
The terror is to be known, completely.
Witches have been burnt at the stake for much less;

Dionysus is continually torn to shreds for his horns
and his eighth notes.

Yes, we are the Grizzly. And Red Riding Hood's Wolf.

You have been forgiven, as a matter of course,

and I am feasting on the sacrificial lamb
we slaughtered, together,
all by myself.

Yet, your future lovers
-- and there will be thousands--
beg me not to let you forget
this One transgression,
even if it was also your most selfless gift:
the courage to push fledglings
over the edge of the cliff
so we can fly on our own.

This is why I am writing this poem
and pasting it on the wind.

The Frog Prince

"My last girlfriend broke up with me because
she didn't like me urinating on her in the shower,"

he said offhandedly as he was turning on my
faucets, testing the water temperature
on the back of his hand,
the one with the bruised knuckles.

This was my date. He lived in the dark.
I was only a tourist there; a cultural anthropologist
conducting a botched auto-ethnography
experiment.

I opened my mouth to ask him why
he seemed surprised by that,
and he reached over and grabbed
a pair of my panties off the tiled floor
and shoved them between my teeth and pulled
my head back by my shocked hair and bent
my inverted swan neck back and bit me hard,
Dracula style.

Excuse me I said, which came out as
"Ehuooosmahhhhhh" as I tried to spit my pink bikinis
out and keep from choking...
Is this what my mother was thinking
when she used to say to me as a child,
"Make sure you wear clean undies
because you never know when you will be caught with
your pants down? [your throat?]

My fear leap-frogged over revulsion, confusion and
something new -- humiliation.
Before I could remark this wasn't what I had in mind
when I invited him over for apple pie and tea and
a discussion on empowerment and feminist theory,
the Marquis De Sade's twenty-first century protege
stripped down to his fruit of the looms.

"There is *one* thing you should know about me and I'll
understand if it causes you to turn away..."
I looked at the hairbrush he was smacking into his free
hand, and remembered how he had bragged he could
turn any Home Depot or Walgreen's product
into a weapon of torturous
pleasure.

"The other woman I'm seeing,
the one I lashed last night with my leather whip until
she bled and then slept with after our date
-- only because you wouldn't come home with me
after the party -- she doesn't care, about my, um,
condition.
But, given that you're so so 'vanilla,'
I thought I'd better give you the option,
instead of surprising you in the dark..."

Here he dramatically pulled down his underpants,
to reveal a penis covered from head to balls
in warts.

"Yes," I said, "No."
I agreed with him on the flavor,
but not on the taste test.

I was glad to have an excuse to end this nonsense
as if all the other reasons were not reason enough.
I threw him his clothes,
and gave him the stiletto boot out the door.

It's been ten years since that day, ten years
since I saw the black-eyed man who worshipped
ocelots

who ordered food for me on our first date without
asking what I wanted
to eat, which made me laugh hysterically,
and say repeatedly, "You're kidding, right?"
Until I began to question if he wasn't only play-acting
the dom. He had only responded with a look of pained
confusion, "You don't like your chicken piccata?"

I don't even remember his name,
my unconsummated S&M fling:
we never slept together;
never even finished a "scene."

But sometimes,
sometimes in the middle of the night,
in the middle of me,
I remember how he would kiss me as gently
as a swan gliding on a pond,
as sweetly as a kitten lapping cream,
then bite my lip so hard I'd gasp
and the air would fill the lungs of some wild animal
and he'd hush me by thrusting his expert tongue deep
inside my mouth and the hot blood
would rise to the surface of every vessel
and we'd float down some strange river

that forked into forbidden streams and swamps
slithering with life forms I never imagined or wished
on anyone and I can't help but wonder what,
what would have happened next...
what would I have *allowed* to happen next...
if he hadn't of had a commutable
bull frog
in his pants?

Would I have ended up a crime statistic, croaking
for more or falling
in love?

To some,
same thing.

Withdrawing the Final Projection

When the mirror has cracked,
when the last image sucked back
into the succubus of our own souls,
ONENESS shatters into a zillion shards.
Jesus packs up his cross and leaves town,
Buddha falls off his thrown and crumbles
into a heap of antique gold dust.

Do you know what its like to be a frigid corpse
sleep-talking among the rubble of love?

I am nothing but a distant ghost.
The white eagle circles 'round my crown of thorns,
yanking at my transparent earlobes with her talons,
but my feet are fading into the quick sand.
If I make a move up or down
I'll be cut in half and lost forever
in a middle-world of torn.

If this is the price of wholeness,
I'm not buying it.

Who would have known withdrawing projections
could cause the genocide

of the whole human race?

Eight billion people's blood on my hands
and all of it my own.

Suddenly, a light sneaks through a crack
onto the back of a pink earthworm.
He is the only one who wants to kiss me now,
and I, in my bitter loneliness
long for even this succulence
like Renfield, Dracula's psychotic lover,
longs for union with that which licks the marrow
from decaying bones.

But alas, there I go, almost tricked again!
Even this blind, boneless beast is but a piece of
projective transference, a shadow
of my own underworld squirmings.
I would only be sucking my own
maggot lips
and putting my tongue
into my own compost.

Besides,
my mouth is already dripping
with worms.

Part IV: Swallow Me, Holy

I would love to kiss you.
The price of kissing is your life.
Now my loving is running toward my life
shouting,
What a bargain, let's buy it!

~ Rumi

You First

I asked a chipmunk to speak to me of love;
    he froze in fear, then darted away.

I asked the well to reveal her depths to me;
    she just stared,
    then splashed water in my face.

I tore at the robes of the Beloved
begging him to answer my prayers,
    and he said,

"Take off your clothes
and offer your own nakedness to the forest.

Only then we can begin
    to negotiate."

El Pollo Loco

On the way to El Pollo Loco
I ran a red light as I was composing
a love poem to God.

When the police man pulled me over and asked,
"Ma am, do you know what you have done?"
I confessed to having drunk too much
of the Holy Spirit
(and stealing metaphors from Sufi poets.)

Something in my eyes
must have moved him
because he stumbled a bit,
laid down his weapon on the street curb
and asked, shyly, if he could have a taste
from the same flask
from which I had been drinking.

I looked deep into his dark eyes and whispered,
"The jail houses are full
of divine lovers tonight."

He gave himself a sobriety test

failed,
and handcuffed himself to my soul.
We drove off together
in his moonlight-drenched patrol car
sipping poetry
as we went in search
of the holy bars.

Serve Me

I am done
with hiding
like the ground hog
who has to wait
365 yo-yo throws of the moon
to have his day
in the sun.

I am done
with wearing
the Emperor's New Clothes
when my own birthday suit
fits like a glove.

I am done with cliches (almost)
with masks and titles worn
like suits of armor;
I am done with subterfuge and tall tales:
all those lies we tell others
to deceive ourselves.

I am done
being anything

but a golden eagle,
a pterodactyl
or a fractal representing
the Cosmos.

And I am so well done
pretending my love
is small like an ant
when it is in fact
a herd of stampeding elephants.

I am done cooking
and ready to be served

to the Gods.

Chalice of Milk

What if it is the nature of a grain of sand
to be swept away?
Would you worry
that it may go too far out to sea?

Would you complain if the ample cow gave too much
milk?
Or accuse the comet of shooting too brightly
across the fated milky way?

Are you stressed that the bee might just suck
too much nectar from the milkweed,
and in a fit of intoxicated desire,
wreak havoc on the hive?

Are you concerned that life itself
might just be too alive?

What if it is, quite simply,
a *woman's* nature
to be swept away
when her shoreline falls in love with the tide,
or her chalice of buttermilk

over

flows,

or her heavenly body glows

when she is stung by the hornet of lust

or becomes rightly drunk

on the nectar of the Gods?

Why be afraid of her currents or her thirst

when we were all born

from the same salt

and loam?

If you won't sip from her holy cup,

at least skim the cream from your own.

Divine Pact

I made a pact with the Devil:
I promised to love him, no matter what.
In return,
he promised nothing.
I kept my promise.
Of course, being the Devil,
he broke his.

I mad a pact with an angel.
I promised to love him, no matter what.
In return
he promised to love the Devil.
Of course, being an Angel,
he kept that promise.

I made a pact with God.
I promised to love him, no matter what.
In return, he promised to love the Angel and the Devil.
Of course being God, he both kept
and broke
his promise.

The Devil, the Angel, God:
these are all names of the Beloved,

and they are all names
the Beloved calls me
depending on which promises
I am keeping
and breaking.

All Our Great Loves

All our great loves shape us
as the ocean carves the shore.

It doesn't matter if we are sand swirling in the tide
or a distant hilltop eroding away
as the cliffs cleaved by waves
meet us in the downslide.

It doesn't matter if our lovers walk us down the isle,
or race us for the Tourist Trophy
'round the Isle of Man,
or pass us on the street as strangers,
or leave us lonely on some deserted shore.

It doesn't matter if what we love is what we eat;
oysters, chocolate, beef stew or fondue;
or what we pet, or mend, or make or grow:
our gardens, houses, quilts, kit cars, wine
or children.

Tend these as if they are the only nourishment
you will ever feast upon, because they are.
Don't wait for the chopped liver
or chrysanthemums

to love you back.

Don't let resentments rise up like weeds
or poison the soil with "what ifs" or "whys."
Love comes not from questions
about the returnings of the water,
but from the yearnings of the sand --
each grain longs to be drowned by its own desire:
that longing is its own wetness.

We only need glimpse the sea to dive
into our salty imaginings,
And then it is only ever our own harbors
we take safe refuge in.

A lover once said, "I think it is better to love
than to be loved, and I fear my affection for you
is shallower than yours."
This made me sad, of course,
until I realized my own love extends
the entire western shoreline.

All those dolphins and whales,
electric eels and sea lions undulating
in the undercurrents
are mine.

If God Gets Lost

What if God
stopped believing
in himself?

What if he
stopped believing
in us?

That's why we must believe
in him no matter what:

to lead him back home
if he ever gets lost.

Now the God*dess*,
she's a different story, altogether.

She would simply ask
for directions.

Dreaming the Garden of Eden

It was such a beautiful dream.
A loving, grief-stricken dream.
Planting the Garden of Eden
witnessing the birth of creation
the original syntax
of form, image and sentience.

We touched the face of god
felt the caress on our own cheek
made love to the devil
who broke our hearts mercilessly
until he felt the break of his own flute
which allowed the pouring in of son light
and inner child tears
fire and water forging the figure of silver bullet
and gold deeper than butter, softer than sunlight
once lost but now found in a w/hole
where we buried and married
the mantis/as/us of ourselves
and wrote four names in the shifting sands of time:
Animas, Animus, Satan, Sutnam:
in the grace of God go we.
This was a garden teaming with spiders,
snakes, cats, mountain lions;

we crawled in the tracks of Elk, Sloth, Lizard, Horse
those winged nightmares and scaled monsters
of earth, sky and water.
We floated down the River Styx, night's blackest sea
drowned and rose up as angels apprenticing
to the voice of the Sun,
the eyes of the Moon,
the body of the Council of Elders.

We listened so deeply to the messages
that our ears began to grow roots,
rooting out the truth that we really are each person
of every day or night dream.
Oh Euripides would have been proud of the unfolding
of a psychodrama more tragic and comic
than even Shakespeare could have dreamed in this
theater of the round
stage of the living room of our future house,
the one we will build over histories' bones,
the place where we will play and plant gardenias
in the backyard of our souls,
haunting and possessing the dispossessed
and blooming into bodies which house
our loving ghosts.
How awkwardly and gracefully we danced
our adolescent dance of celebration

of courtship between the archetypal Gods
painfully together, painfully alone
we rode the archaic carousel of Mandalas
tried to burn that which we refused to own
that which could not be burned,
but rather transformed into a healthier,
initiated form of terror,
love, desire, fear, confusion
circling us counter-clockwise
across boundaries
over east and west's treacherous bridges
which broke and sent us plummeting
into brackish waters
surrendering,
opening,
submitting to the downward spiral,
which looped strangely
into the other direction of eternity
as the trickster switched symbols on us
and the sun escaped from prison
as it rained before it snowed
gracing us with a weather report
of our own souls.

How often we saw the man behind our own masks,
peered through one black and one blue contact lens,

cracked glasses -- rose-colored bifocals --
taped in the middle
made laughable
which opened the door for Joy
our long lost friend,
to fly into the arms of our hearts once more
and sing songs which could not be sung out-loud
but were hummed relentlessly and selfishly
and burned into our beings with a musical
cattle prod
at the edges of our awareness.

Oh, I know this was all a figment
of my fragmented imagination,
a fantasy of universal proportions and importance,
of healing, desire, genealogy, names, signs, sacred
contracts and vows.

Now I fear with the upmost grief and trepidation
this was only illusion:
wishful thinking,
the sickest and cruelest joke Satan could make
or the simple ravings of lunatics
who cannot bear a life without magic and love
and meaning anymore.

And yet, even if this is only fantasy,
a trick of hypnotic suggestion,
I must love her anyway,
this dream of pomegranate seeds and forbidden apples.
For her rose-colored scent is so sweet,
her promise of budding seeds so seductive
her words so profound and profane they could never be
uttered in the light of day
and may even be too sublime to bare within the open
wound of night.

I began this dream
in the galley of a pirate ship, a free man
and now I bind myself to you God,
to Mantas my own soul and yes
to the phantom who keeps penetrating
my being in the middle of the night.
No matter how real or illusory,
I give myself over to the underworld and the upper
and yes, even in Middle Earth
in the name of angelic slavery;
This is the only way to be free.

Hear the beat of my drum, Mother Earth,
you who can no longer speak for yourself.
I will listen to your death rattle of crickets,

of wind moaning through the cracks of me
with the help of this gift of sound
found in my red and golden sack
bought on Pluto's shores
woven by the hands of a master weaver
who died his own yard with the colors of his beloved
Crete.

I will hold this drum stick fiercely and gently
the one carved from the Tree of Life
whose roots descend
into the kiva of our bodies
into the spirit hole
into the primordial oozes,
into the chthonic center
where our origins beckon with music and fingers
whose touch is so painfully sweet and maddening
in their infinite caressing
only ancient beings who have died many times
can endure the terror of her womb,
and join in the primal cries of her lion's song.
If only you will speak them to me,
I will deliver your sacred messages across the lost
borders of reality.

My legs are weak. I stumble and crawl

like a human infant,
or a newborn chick with egg on her face.

But my eyes!
My eyes see through the yoke,
eyes that are brighter than the sun
and crazed like those of a wolf alone in the deep night
almost murdered by her prey
licking the red blood of the fresh kill off the driven
snow; I howl the only song re-membered
from my dogged childhood:

"Row, row, row your (pirate) boat
gently down the stream,
Merrily, murderously, miraculously
("Merchants for terrible, terrible things, Ha!)
Life is but a dream"

And I will never wake up again
which is to say without words
"I am awake and will never go back to sleep!"
For I am the word stuck in your throat
I am the world that loves you back
I am the black witch
the white wanderer
the grey web weaver betrothed

in a deranged marriage
to the great weaver of us all:
the president, the roommate, the sister, the brother, the
child, the lover
the bored of directors
the guardian of the western soul
whose name, whose gift, whose passion and purpose
whose life's vision
is first and foremost
to dream.

Magnum Opus:
Invocation of a Museful Marriage
Composed for Laura and Tom's Wedding, April 2012

Oh how the muses are excited today!
They are hoping you will find your way
into the secret
wedding chapel of your soul
and whisper sweetly to them,
or bellow
for all the world to hear
"I do!"

Can you hear them right now?
Humming and giggling in the eves,
holding hands and playing a game called "Trust."
See them leaning back and twirling
round and round
enraptured
until dizzily they fall to earth
and break through new ground.
Oh hear them moaning,
at the pangs caused by crashing and desire;
hear them squealing with delight
at their own animal sounds,

then running up the steps of each other's laughter.

The music of emotion beats with giant wings.
It is the sound of them making love
and their love-making is an excavation machine:
they are always mining gold within themselves
to forge into gifts the shape of wedding rings
and rings of trees: the inner circle-dance of saplings
and mandalas of the ancient greens,
the roundness of new growth and longevity.

When love is chiseled into marriage
and marriage is framed into a perpetual work of art
life becomes a masterpiece
far beyond anything Pachelbel or Michael Angelo or
the Angels playing trumpets in the Sistine Chapel
could create.

This one is already a mixed media extravaganza
of sewing thread and patterned cotton,
light and celluloid,
kitty purrrrs and Dreamfish lured
to the Eleusinian mysteries and explosions
of white calla lilies, sunflowers, sisters
and brothers.

This ode must be sung *even* in a sink
full of dirty dishes;
danced especially on the desk
where there are bills to pay.
It is a concerted effort,
an unfurling symphony
with notes that can burst into blossoms
scented with the roses and resin
of violin strings.

This love will devastate the world
with it wild beauty
like the Moon's reflection skinny-dipping
in a mountain stream,
a honeymoon in Italy,
or the singing of the Song of Songs of Solomon.
Its only goal is to surrender to itself
and make all those with petrified hearts
fall to their knees and weep.

And even though this sacred collage
is sure to be museum quality
take it to the streets!

Scribble it on the sidewalks like the chalk drawings
your future children will play hop scotch on.

Throw away your fine, brittled brushes
and finger paint it:
get your hands messy and your feet stained
like the glorious wine makers who make us drunk
by squashing grapes intimately between their toes,
and the potters who kneed and stroke the body
of the Earth and the first Gods
who fashioned man and woman
from clay, and dust.

You MUST parade your romance through the city
like a Mardi Gras or circus act,
riding on the back of prancing elephants or in a car
impossibly full of clowns.

Spray your devotion like rebellious graffiti
in the subway.
Hold it up on the street corner as a sign
of the most profound social protest,
then perform it in theatrics
of insane symbolic revelation.
Wear your love like tribal body art.
Tattoo it on your chest, like a warrior's totem
that emboldens him on the battlefield,
and accompanies her in death.

Then, in times of darkness,
you will know exactly how to weave
the light of your faith, your trust, your shining hope
into a magical tapestry: this
flying quilt will carry you
through the blackest thunder clouds
over the brightest rainbows.

And when you reach the other side,
carve monuments of stone to each other's
accomplishments;
then, carve soft bowls, or barrels, to collect the rain
that will inevitably fall from your eyes during times
of sorrow, and bliss.

Drink this!

For the wetness of the body
is the nectar of the Gods:
make offerings of each other's salt
to Neptune and the albatross.

Finally,
craft a sailboat out of truthfulness;
erect a triple mast in homage
to the Son, the Father and the Holy Ghost,

a vessel so divine in its magnificence
it will glide through any argument, any tempest
and charm the whales and the mermaids
into revealing their siren songs;
treasures for your endless repertories.

This kind of creative marriage
is what Artemis was, after.
A quiver large enough
to hold all her golden arrows,
and room enough for her friend Athena's owl
to lay viscous eggs in.
Let this gigantic nest
be your pantheon and your unity;
applaud it always, for what it is,
at every flight of every feather,
at every weigh and every measure:
your *Magnum Opus*;
Your Greatest Work.

Even the muses will be amused
on *this* playground
of unconditional love.

Photosymphony

Written for the Santa Barbara Symphony Orchestra, 2010

In the concert hall of time
a cacophony of crickets and coyotes,
crooning babies and percolating coffee makers,
morning doves and bees sipping jasmine
tune the dawn.

The World yawns, stretches
opens the proscenium curtain to reveal
Earth's conductor lifting up her wand.
Morning turns his spot light on,
sunlight bursts into frenzied song.

A stanza of manic seagulls
lures us from our land-locked beds:
we transcend
to endless measures of California shoreline
glimmering like tanning oil
on the curves of a lover.
Surfers ride these glistening glissandos
while clefs treble and
crescendos crash against reverberating cliffs.
The sun drips off the satin backs of dolphins
arpeggioing through emerald waters.

On the salty marsh,
a hummingbird trills,
her iridescent wings messaging
clandestine rhymes to a dragonfly
who secrets back
staccatto'd fire flashes
as he dive bombs silvery streams
rich with fins
that beckon hope
to fishermen
like sirens' grins
or mermaid fugues.
Even the wise succumb
to the gold of fools,
etudes of abalone shell,
and the glare of a child's pinwheel long abandoned in
the sand.
These are lost pirate treasures
and the flutes of pied pipers.

Sparkles flirt with us
like bioluminescence
and the moon's reflection rising
on a Gypsy's violin.
They dig their glinting blade in us
like day dreams yet unlived.

On the golden meadow,
white rabbits appear
and disappear
down magic wholes
while obsidian grows its' slowly pace
and turtles, bones and amethysts
rest in grasses in between
the expanding dappled shade.
A chorus of photosynthesis
gives rise to unfurling seeds,
those left-handed eighth notes
that will explode into a melody
of vociferous daisies
in the final movement.

Over Pan's amphitheater,
crowds of crows and clouds gather,
fretting in antithesis.
Thunder beats his darkening drum,
Zeus's cymbals crash unsung.
Now, at climax of storm and sun
the Diva of damp borderlands
opens up her arms to expand
her rainbow-colored accordion.

The ravens go crazy.

The condors rip-roaringly applaud
(inadvertently bringing Tinker Bell back to life.)
The rain bows in all her glory
to a standing ovulation.
The Maestro gives birth right then and there
to illumination; it dawns on her
The Ancients had danced it right
all along
in the mosh pit of imagination:

The Sun is Divine:
and we are each and every one of us
instruments of light.

Love Letter to Earth

Composed at Esalen Retreat Center, CA April 6, 2012

Dear Earth:

I love you.
I have loved you since that time
near Big Pine, California, at the Obsidian Mine
where I felt a vision in my loins
and sunk into the hot core of you
and sunk into the womb of everyone
and felt our heart beating in unison:
the heart of One
exquisite, ever-unfolding being.

I have loved you since I learned to tie my shoes
which I did
and undid, countless times
so as to run my toes through your lovely green hair.
That was the summer I trespassed
into the neighbor's yard and stepped
on a fallen star, that had prickles.
My mother trespassed at my urging too
and declared it a "weed."
But I was not fooled:
"Weed" is the medicine name for "Star!"

The ancient neighbor agreed.
When I asked him why he collected rain water
in a wooden barrel
he looked at me with astonishment and cried
"Why, these are God's tears!"
It was only years later I discovered the truth:
they are!

Dearest Earth, I've love you as far back as yesterday
when you showed me how a blade of grass quivers
like a violin string
and how every seed unfurls to perfection
like a woman's inner beauty
and a man's humanity.
I love you, now
tonight
for all your opposites:
your gravity and levity
your goldfinch wings and swirling leaves,
your heat and cold,
rocks and mold,
your tea roses, cinnamon toast, lavender soap and stink
weed. I love you for your dirt and dew,
your stems and sticky stamens
your loopty loops.
I love you for your bark and bitter,

your nectar flowing,
your honey, your sugar.

In summation, Earth:
I love your culmination.
I love your signs and symbols, your unsolved mysteries,
your astounding synchronicities.
I love you for the dreams you send
the griefs you take
and the lullabies your oceans make
as I lay my head down to sleep
on your chest rising and falling
in the wake
of another glorious morning.

Reply From the Earth
Channeled at Esalen Retreat Center, CA April 7, 2012

Dear Beloved,

I see you.
I have watched you in every season
at every hour
of every day.

I have watched your fingers, sinew, pulses, nose:
every languid, moaning, wanting
fluctuation of your body
and all its inclinations, ruminations, and devastations.

I have roamed every hall
of your unfathomable imagination,
and live now to tell about it.

I imagine you:

Your hilltops yodeling drunken goats
your caverns dank and dripping
with underground streams,
overflowing with little fishes
that speak to my fishes

(they go to school together.)

I feel you.

Your quiverings and undulations
your shimmerings and glimmerings
your hesitations and restraints.
Within my own body I lean into your
poses, postures, postulations,
falling forwards
and retreats.
I pulse to your heart throbbing;
your magic drumbeats.

I know you.
Your coyotes and your lynx.
Your lizards, alligators, turtles and jaguars
your whales, seals and minx.
I know your raccoon and your mouse,
your lion with thorns,
your prickly pears, your pruning shears,
your lawn mower
and every inch worm
of your secret garden.

And finally,

I AM YOU
And you are me,
and together we are all and everything
that has ever been or will ever be:
I am your mouth
your ears
your rising sun
your fullest moon
and all the wonders in between.

I LOVE YOU
AND YOU LOVE ME.

The Home We Never Made Together

I know now, why,
Fate refused to let us live together.
We would have sat content and warm
at our cozy hearth,
lost in each other's I's.
Blind to the frosted window pain,
deaf to the wind begging,
the tree branches frantically jumping up and down
trying to get our attention...failing;
the broken teeth of the world chattering
cold and forlorn.

I know now why
we could never allow our insatiable desire
to be satisfied. The world needs our fire!
The one that burns eternally
in the basement of the home
we never made together.
That furnace is why
we were born.

Love may be tinder
but yearning is coal.

The Dreamweaver

I met myself last night.
She smiled.
I screamed.

"I am the Dreamweaver," she exclaimed
and showed proof of her weaving:

In the dream she is holding up the hood
of my car with her torso, which has a head
but no limbs
(which is how I feel after ten hours of writing.)

She looks like a re-membered image
from a Salvador Dali painting,
-- though I can't remember what the image is --
and the painting of a woman,
an artist's model wearing a jockey's hat
that my Grandmother painted
(who may be dying.)

and this reminds me of other dreams where
I was befriending the Dali Lama
whom I met at his temple in Dharmsala,

and also seductive Indian women.

As I looked at the woman's face, it changed
and became the face of the artist
who has been painting all of my dreams,
and worse, my nightmares.
She didn't want to scare me
– or perhaps she did --
but she compensated by giving me other dreams
of men who massage my feet
and make promises of trips to Europe,
(which are sometimes preferable
to the trips themselves.)
She is kind in that way,
though terrible in others,
not meaning to be,
but being whom she is,
"The Dreamweaver"
connected to this side
of my consciousness by a silver thread,
one that runs strong as a bull through to the other side
of my soul, which is your soul,
the Soul of the World.
God is holding on to the end of that leash....
No, God is the leash!
No wonder I trembled at the hand that holds

and tried to run from her, from him, from us.

How can I go on in the way that I have
having seen her face
and recognizing it as my own?

My mirror is different today,
and so is the world,
for I know she has been coming out
to play and work
not only in my dreams
but in my poems,
my letters, fantasies, and loving.

She is the Spider,
the Spinner,
the one who makes me dizzy,
the one who leads me around on a short leash
to meet kindred spiders
who weaves webs of synchronicity
around my nail-bit fingers
in order to catch flies,
which is to say,
to show us all how to fly.

She is a Sculptor of sacred images.

She is a rebel who rails against other sculptors
imprisoning her in alabaster.

She is the one who gives up arms
yet still seems to knows how to knead
the clay that is the collective
with whatever body parts remains.

I went to Borders today
and found the familiar, forgotten painting
right away in the art section of Master Works.
It is Salvador Dali's "Hallucination of the Toreador."
Look at it one way, you see the repeated image
of the Venus de Milo,
the feminine who loves and gives birth.
Pierce deeper into her
and you will see the image of El Matadore,
He Who Loves
To The Death.

Eric

I want to write a love poem for you
but how does one describe another
who is as close as her own skin and
as much a part of her
as her own happiness?
It's been so long since I have known suffering
within the context of love, my thundercloud
of words has given way to turquoise sky.
I have to find a brighter color ink,
or give up writing for dancing.

There are no metaphors for the Sun.
The candle's glow, the lightening bug, a forest fire;
all fail to illuminate luminescence.

There is no way to tell of the sharpness
of the sword blade, the dagger or the glare that cuts
when your eyes tell me I have let down
both of us.

There is no way to explain the sweetness of sugar
except to place it on a hungry tongue --
and yes, I do get jealous when the skinny blondes
open their mouths and look your way, licking their lips

in my imagination, or on your Facebook page.
Hera was always jealous in regard to Zeus
and although you certainly are no God,
you know I worship you like one.

I could easily write about the dozen fights we've had:
the carton of eggs cracking and
the gourmet omelets we made out of them.
I could document the electric arcs sparked by our fifty
arguments over politics and religion, which ignited
our shared passion for truth and justice.
I could write about the quiet frustration that has settled
like dust over our messy house,
or of the running of the bills.
I could still wax poetic about the one winter
of our discontent: although we've sealed the inevitable
betrayal with candle wax, the flame of anger still burns
on silently in the ice cave of the distant past.

But to write about the other 2,800 days of sunshine;
the 56,000 hours (yes, I counted)
of azures seas sailed upon,
of blue birds singing in our kitchen;
of eating hotdogs and popcorn with our super heros
in dark caverns; of fringe and foreign characters

lounging in our living room; of wild dreams and desires
fulfilled again and again in the tangled sheets,
of trips laced
with music and nature and slot machines
to Vegas, Taft, Sedona, San Francisco, Yosemite, Zion,
the property we bought on Ebay for $1,000 at the edge
of the Grand Canyon we still can't find, and
our primitive cabin you call a shed in Alaska;
of one thousand red and yellow and pink roses
and ten thousand oranges dripping from branches
of the tree house we live in here in Santa Barbara...

Immortalizing our lives together in syllables and
numbers
is a task only someone like Shakespeare, DH Lawrence,
the Bronte Sisters, Rogers and Hammerstein, Bob Dylan
or Sir Isaac Newton could accomplish.

So, I'll give up trying to trace the constellations
and just say plainly:
I'm glad our lives are intertwined
like the winged caduceus.
You are snake
but also swan.

And I love every one of your scales and feathers.

There, I said it

It only took me 14,154 words
to work up the courage and express
"I love you" to those I love.

God help us,
and the trees
and the elves inside the printing press
if I ever try to tell you why,
or have to say

"Goodbye."

(Sequel soon to be at Amazon.)

Acknowledgments

At first, I planned to thank only those who *directly* inspired the poems in this book: the knights in rusty armor, the Micky Mouse sorcerers who brought mad broom sticks to life in the fantasia of my heart. But as soon as I began to invite in gratitude, the room filled up with a party of other lovely ghosts. So while these poems may point to specific transformational peaks, devastations and epiphanies, or address a particular lover encountered in some distant, enchanted forest, they all begin and end in the same village where my dearest friends and family dwell.

It is only now, as my poems are finally working their way into the sunlight, that I am beginning to understand how the seeds of all growth, of all poetry, have been watered by those who helped tend our garden of dreams. Without this sustenance from others, our souls wither; our ink wells would dry up. Thankfully, the love of those surrounding me does not fill a watering can, but rather, an ocean basin. So eternal gratitude to:

Nedra and Bob Katz, my soulful parents.

Traci Young, Aliza Kaim, Pam Burnt, Michelle Freed Bulgatz, Robin Graham, Lisa Abramowitz, Caren Linn and Penny Line, my childhood friends and partners in creative mayhem.

Debra Katz, my dazzling twin and inspiration (you're two books ahead, but I'm catching up!) and Brad Katz, the sweetest and funniest brother I know, who helped design the cover of this book.

Mrs. Grek-Cooper, we wouldn't be who we are today without you: the perfect grammar school English teacher who let us burn our grammar books and start the Edgar Allan Poe reading group and school newspaper at age twelve.

My role models in the art of love, or at least, endurance: Christine Russell, Dale Sollow, Dotty Katz, Dale & Carolyn Lauderdale, my next-best-thing to parents.

Marian Fuentes, Laura Pagano, Tami Silicio, Ann Marie Molnar, Jeff Bile, the Wardlaw-Baileys, Keith Himebaugh, Cat Brown, Terry West, Bob Egan, Aradhna Malik, Mirela Albertson, Will Coley, Princess Williams, Rachel, Roxy and Manny Katz, the Lauderdales: Hannah, Andrea, Rob, Jacob, Owen, Greg, Brian and Sarah; the Goldfines: Larry, Lisa, Jamie, Brian, Jeff and Michael: my heros, all.

Of course I am indebted to the acclaimed poets who made me fall in love with poetry: Mother Goose, Shakespeare, Dr. Seuss, Rumi, Shel Silverstein, Hafiz, T.S. Elliot, Charles Dickens, Charles Bukowski, Ray Bradbury, Anne Sexton, Rilke, Mary Oliver, Marge Piercy, David Whyte.

Infinite thanks to my true loves and underworld guides. You reminded me how to love myself, and thus how to care for the "Animus Mundi," the Soul of the World:

Eric Lauderdale, my now and forever.
Norman, my first and always.
Dave Montgomery, my co-guide and ever-flowering Tree.
Don Motz, my "Synergy," Moose, my "Security;"
Frank Q., my "Happy Otter."

Special thanks to Stephen Aizenstat, Arny Mindell, Gary Toub and Elaine Molchanov, my "dreamy" mentors and depth psychology gurus. Also Emerald North, Tom Brown Jr.,

Jade Shearer, Trebbe Johnson, Moriah Vecchia, Anne Stein, Gigi Coyle and Angelo Lazenka: you helped me recover my mythic voice and desire to follow in your footsteps, in the moccasins of our ancestors.

To Bill Plotkin, the exquisite owl whose tender lizard so wildly captivated my imagination: thank you for shadow dancing with me in the banquet hall of mirrors.

It was all of you, along with my fellow questers, dreamtenders, beloved clients and warrior students -- all those whom I have ever been blessed to nestle with in the cupped palms of sacred council -- who helped me hear the poetry of every-day speech and to perceive the "ordinary magic" of nature (our nature.) To sum up the gestalt of what I learned from you, and what I will spend my life teaching others:

We are born poets.
Life is one extraordinary, collective, epic poem.
The Earth is our sacred manuscript; we must tend it as the holiest of scriptures.

Finally, to my editor, to myself:
thank you for having the courage to publish this first chapter of my soul.

And finally, to the *Great Publisher In the Sky:*
Infinite thanks, for publishing us all.

Sincerely Yours,

The Lizard Thief

About the Cover Photo

Michael Turco's photograph, taken on June 19th, 2003, shows a Florida Burrowing Owl (Athene cunicularia floridana) consuming a Green Iguana (Iguana iguana.) It is the first scientific documentation of the reciprocally predatory relationship between these two species (apparently, they eat each other.) These gorgeous iguanas are an exotic species originating from Central and South America, which up until this picture was taken, were believed to be the prey of only two other species: the domesticated dog and the Yellow-crowned night heron. But on this day, the male owl was seen feeding the lizard to his chicks in their underground burrow. Ironically, researchers from Florida Atlantic University had been studying the area because they feared the Iguanas might be stealing and eating the nesting owls' eggs: leading to the further demise of the protected species. Burrowing owls are the only owls known to be active during the day.

Photographer Michael Turco is a big-hearted steward of the Earth who specializes in nature photography that advances biological and ecological research/education. His stunning images span the Globe from the Amazon to Africa to the Everglades, and appear in National Geographic Explorer, National Geographic Kids, Bird Watchers Digest, Discover, American Forests, and numerous other journals, books and calendars. Please visit his website to obtain copyright permissions, and to see more of his stunning collaborations with nature:

www.agpix.com/michaelturco

(Reference: Florida Field Naturalist 33(4):125-127, 2005 and Mike Turco, correspondence.)

About the Type Face

The text in the body of each poem is printed in **Optima**, a sans serf linotype created by Hermann Zapf in 1950. As the legend goes, the obsessed engraver was visiting the Basilica di Santa Croce, a medieval church in Florence, Italy, and happened upon an ancient Roman gravestone that had mysterious letters cut into the epitaph. Intrigued and inspired by the classical design, Zaph returned to Germany where he spent two years crafting the noble font into metal.

Both the Vietnam Memorial in Washington DC, and the September 11th memorial in New York City, called "Reflecting Absence," memorializes the names of the fallen heros in Optima.

The titles are set in *Cochin (bold/italic.)* This is a traditional serif typeface emblematic of the typographical Neo-renaissance movement. First produced in 1912 by Georges Peignot for the Paris foundry Deberny & Peignot, it was based on the engravings of French artist Nicholas Cochin, born in 1610. He excelled in intricate copper figures, which he infused with life-like animation. His subject matter epitomized war and divinity. Cochin was called the "The Elder" by those in the region who honored his exemplary craftsmanship.

(References: 1. Bryan's Dictionary of Painters and Engravers by Michael Bryan, eds. Robert Edmund Graves and Sir Walter Armstrong, 1886–1889. 2. Zapf, Alphabet Stories, A Chronicle of Technical Developments, Cary Graphic Arts Press, New York, 2008.

About the Author

Amy Beth Katz leads a poetic life. She is a writer of fiction and nonfiction, a visionary rites of passage guide, shamanic healer, nature photographer, social activist, teacher, realtor, publisher and former horse drawn carriage driver. She has lived in nine countries, on four continents -- in war zones, red light districts, mystical art colonies, a sailboat in the Caribbean, and the wilds of Utah.

For the past ten years, Amy has commuted to Anchorage, Alaska, where she teaches relationship skills and public speaking to US service members as part of University of Alaska's military education programs.

When this peace activist is not taking the whip to handsome, obedient men in camouflage, or tracking bears around her primitive cabin in Eagle River, or helping others to claim the wild animals within themselves, she resides among the roses and fruit trees in sunny Santa Barbara, CA. She lives with her boyfriend Eric, a guitar maker/craftsman, and their three loquacious conures.

When Amy grows up, or retires, she hopes to be doing everything she's doing now.

To arrange a poetry reading/book signing, attend a workshop or vision quest, or to schedule a transformational healing session, visit Amy at:

www.livingdreamspress.com
www.schooloflivingdreams.com

Email: amybethkatz@livingdreamspress.com